T0354838

My Diary

With wisdom from "Papa's Letters" for daily meditation

Judith C. Lovell

authorHOUSE

AuthorHouse™
1663 Liberty Drive
Bloomington, IN 47403
www.authorhouse.com
Phone: 1 (800) 839-8640

Published by AuthorHouse 01/22/2020

ISBN: 978-1-7283-4228-3 (sc)
ISBN: 978-1-7283-4227-6 (e)

~

After spending time in meditation and prayer, I commit today to the following:

- (30) thirty consecutive days of writing in my diary making permanent personal testimonies

- selecting a quiet place for writing (somewhere I will NOT be disturbed)

- including in this sacred space - a lit white candle for sustaining inspiration, a small green plant symbolizing growth and development, a cool glass of refreshing water to sip from, a tissue or handkerchief scented with a drop of Rosemary essential oil to inhale encouraging creativity and clear mindedness, a timer, a pen, and my diary

- (1) one minute of writing for the first day, (2) two minutes of writing for the second day, (3) three minutes of writing for the third day, increasing the time spent writing by a minute each day until I have spent (25) twenty-five minutes writing on day 25

- using Papa's words at the top of the page to direct my thoughts through this creative method, I simply write without worrying about spelling or grammatical errors, incomplete thoughts or punctuation

- writing (5) five informal letters – on e on each day from Day 26 through Day 30 enjoying the process

I understand the importance of committing to my emotional, intellectual, and spiritual growth. I therefore, agree to be consistent and dedicated to this powerfully life changing endeavor. As I express myself daily through these writing exercises, I gain a competitive advantage in this Age of Information over those who cannot communicate effectively.

_____   _____
(Print Name)   (Date)

_____
(Signature)

DAY 1

My head is full, my heart is overflowing, my pen is ready, paper is convenient, and ink is nearby: All I have to do is write...

_____

_____

_____

_____

_____

_____

_____

_____

_____

_____

_____

_____

10

DAY 2

Let us think of life, for that is here and now

_____

_____

_____

_____

_____

_____

_____

_____

_____

_____

_____

_____

_____

_____

_____

_____

DAY 3

...I am sure of my ability ~ to secure a livelihood

DAY 4

Of course the world turns round and
conditions change occasionally

_____

_____

_____

_____

_____

_____

_____

_____

_____

_____

_____

_____

_____

DAY 5

Our destiny will work itself out

_____

_____

_____

_____

_____

_____

_____

_____

_____

_____

_____

_____

_____

_____

_____

_____

DAY 6

There is nothing can successfully stop
the mighty rushing flow of love

_____

_____

_____

_____

_____

_____

_____

_____

_____

_____

_____

_____

_____

DAY 7

...by the exercise of the strongest power of will I ultimately succeeded to rid myself of that deep feeling of chagrin

DAY 8

...finally started to make an effort to think over the situation from a reasonable view point

---

DAY 9

But let us hope, and keep on hoping for the best

DAY 10

Well there is nothing on earth ~ or Heaven, for that matter ~ that is as great as love: Nothing that exercises so great an influence upon people as a whole

_____

_____

_____

_____

_____

_____

_____

_____

_____

_____

_____

_____

_____

DAY 11

Life is so hard to live when a person has no one who is interested ~ no one who is concerned ~ no one to commune with ~ no one to confide in

DAY 12

I wish that I was gifted with the

power to work miracles

158

DAY 13

*We have taken the word "can't" from
the English Language entirely and in
its place - we've written "let's try"*

_____

_____

_____

_____

_____

_____

_____

_____

_____

_____

_____

_____

_____

DAY 14

It is therefore necessary for one to observe the strictest economy in his expenditures if he desires to save and keep some money

DAY 15

...it is not what a man (woman) makes
or earns that counts it is what he saves

_____

_____

_____

_____

_____

_____

_____

_____

_____

_____

_____

_____

_____

DAY 16

I am anxious to please

_____

_____

_____

_____

_____

_____

_____

_____

_____

_____

_____

_____

_____

_____

_____

DAY 17

…I am anxious…to encourage

_____

_____

_____

_____

_____

_____

_____

_____

_____

_____

_____

_____

_____

_____

DAY 18

for neglectfulness in this case would amount to cruelty

_____

_____

_____

_____

_____

_____

_____

_____

_____

_____

_____

_____

_____

_____

238

DAY 19

the tender whisperings of Love

DAY 20

I thank you for it

_____

_____

_____

_____

_____

_____

_____

_____

_____

_____

_____

_____

_____

_____

_____

DAY 21

God will bless us this year

DAY 22

With trembling fingers I broke the seal,
and eagerly devoured its contents

_____

_____

_____

_____

_____

_____

_____

_____

_____

_____

_____

_____

_____

_____

_____

_____

278

DAY 23

we all have " faults"

302

DAY 24

I admire your modesty

DAY 25

I can not tell what may happen in years, but just now my only apparent hope for a living, is here-

Congratulations

You did it!

DAY 26

_____

_____

_____

_____:

Thank you for

_____

_____

_____

_____

_____

_____

_____

_____

_____

DAY 27

_____

_____

_____

_____:

Thinking of you

_____

_____

_____

_____

_____

_____

_____

_____

_____

_____

DAY 28

_____

_____

_____

_____:

I release from my life

_____

_____

_____

_____

_____

_____

_____

Day 29

_____

_____

_____

_____:

I forgive you

_____

_____

_____

_____

_____

_____

_____

_____

_____

_____

DAY 30

_____

_____

_____

_____ :

I love you so much

_____

_____

_____

_____

_____

_____

_____

_____

Certificate of Achievement

Awarded to

_____

(Print Your Name)

CONGRATULATIONS!

THIS CONFIRMS THAT THE PERSON NAMED ABOVE HAS SUCCESSFULLY DEDICATED THIRTY DAYS TO WRITING.

ON THIS _____ DAY OF _____. 20_____

Judith C. Lovell
Your Author